RUBANK EDUCATIONAL LIBRARY

RUBANK INTERMEDIATE Method

VIOLA

SYLVAN D. WARD

A FOLLOW UP COURSE FOR INDIVIDUAL OR LIKE-INSTRUMENT CLASS INSTRUCTION

RUBANK®

HAL•LEONARD® CORPORATION

7777 W. BLUEMOUND RD. P.O. BOX 13819 MILWAUKEE, WI 53213

PREFACE

One of the most beautiful sounding orchestral instruments is the Viola.
No other instrument has a tone just like it, and therefore there is
no substitute for it in the modern orchestra. Once the orchestra
has become accustomed to the profound melancholy chant in the
viola's lower strings, and the happy, serene and ethereal beauty
expressed in the upper register, it will never be without this pre-
cious member of the string family.

During the past few years, the viola has earned real popularity.
Violin players usually take a special liking to the instrument. It
is customary for some directors to invite second violin players to
learn the viola before entering the first violin section.

There are a number of fine, rare old violas in existence today.
Some of the most beautiful and famous were made by Gasparo da
Salo (1542 - 1609), Gironimo Amati (1551 - 1635) and Antonio
Stradivarius (1644 - 1737).

The viola is an excellent instrument for solo work, and players
will find a large library of music, including many works by great
masters, from which they can select material suitable for this pur-
pose.

Sylvan D. Ward

The Viola Clef (𝄡)
Also known as the Alto or C Clef

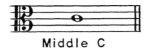
Middle C

You will notice that Middle C appears on the 3rd line in Viola Clef. The Clef is made by taking two lines from the Bass Clef and two lines from the Treble Clef, with Middle C serving as the center line thus:

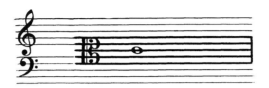

THE VIOLA STRINGS

The strings are tuned in fifths, like the Violin, except that the highest string is A and the lowest is C (a fifth lower than the Violin).

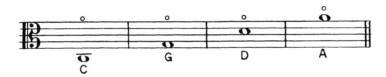

FIRST POSITION NOTES AND FINGERING

Showing the same notes on the Violin in Treble Clef

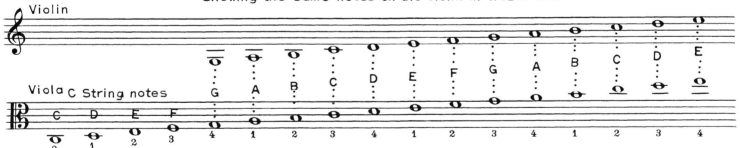

FINGER PLACEMENT
First Position on all Strings

Half Steps are indicated by brackets.

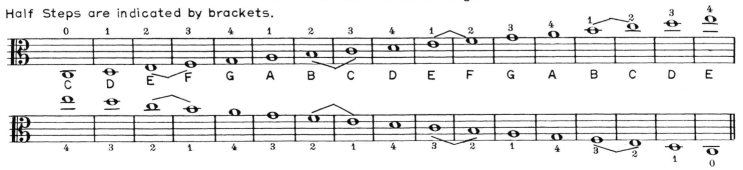

829-47

Scale Fun

Practice first seperate bowing, then 2 in a bow, and finally 4 in a bow.

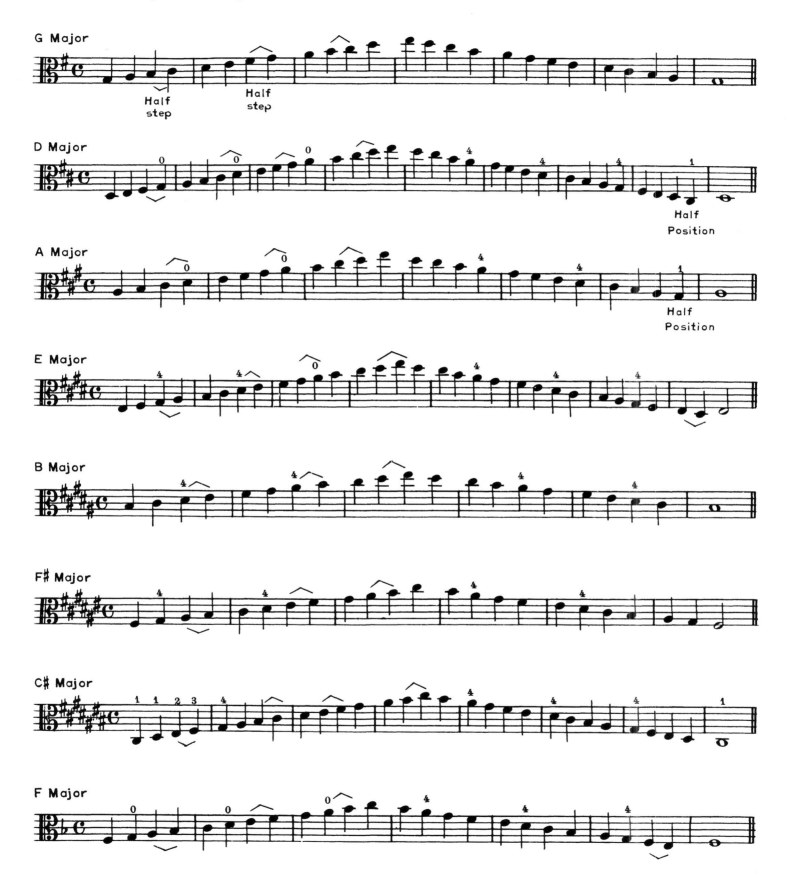

Melodic Minor Scales

Intervals

Name notes before playing.
Practice pizzicato first, then with the bow.

Seconds

Thirds

rit

Fourths

Fifths

✱ Note that the 2nd finger must be drawn back a half step to play F natural after crossing over from B natural on the G String.

8

Intervals (Continued)

Practice three ways: frog, middle and point.

Sixths

Sevenths

Octaves

Ninths

Tenths

Sailing Along

Etude No.1

Moderato

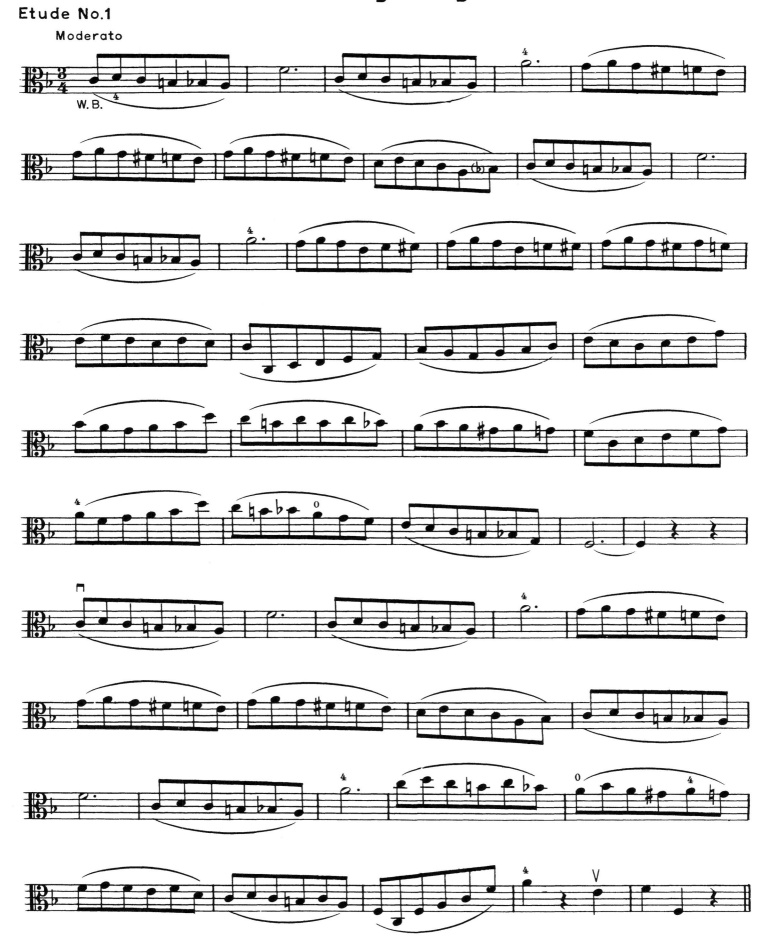

Theme and Variation

Etude No. 2

dim. and rall.

Detached Bowing Melody

Etude No.3

Power in the Bow

Etude No. 4

* Martelé — The bow is moved quickly and stopped abruptly.

* See this and other important bow strokes fully described in the "Instrumental Director's Hand Book" published by Rubank.

The Turn (∾)

The Turn is a form used to represent a group of notes played before or after a note thus:

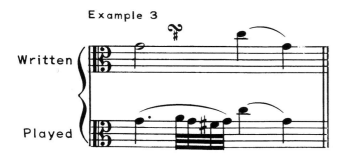
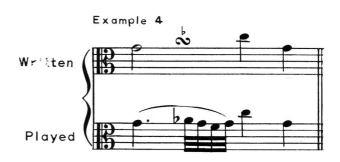

If a sharp is written above the Turn ⸜ the highest note is raised.

If a sharp is written below the Turn ⸝ the lowest note is raised.

If a flat is written, the note would be lowered.

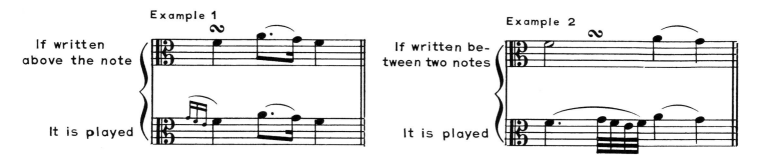

Shepherd's Tune

The Old Spinning Wheel Hums a Tune

Etude No. 5

Note: Also practice the first three lines and last three lines with 8 notes in one bow.

Feathertouch

Etude No. 6

Scherzo

Etude No. 7

The Positions

The positions present no particular problem. They simply represent a method used to extend the range of notes and make otherwise difficult music easy to read. For each consecutive position, the hand is merely moved up the fingerboard one scale degree. It may be either a half step or a whole step, depending upon the key signature or accidentals involved. For example, in the key of C major, the range of notes and fingering in the first, second and third positions would appear as follows:

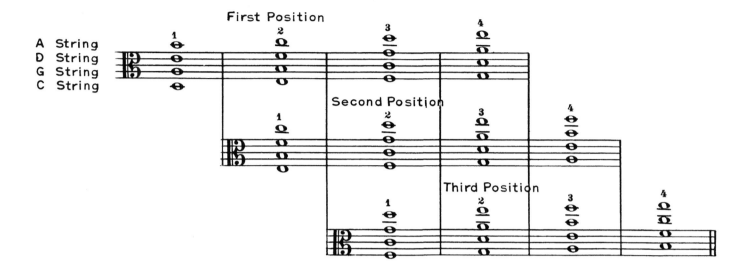

The treble clef (𝄞) is also used in viola music to avoid having to read too many leger lines in viola clef. The names of the lines and spaces in the treble clef are as follows:

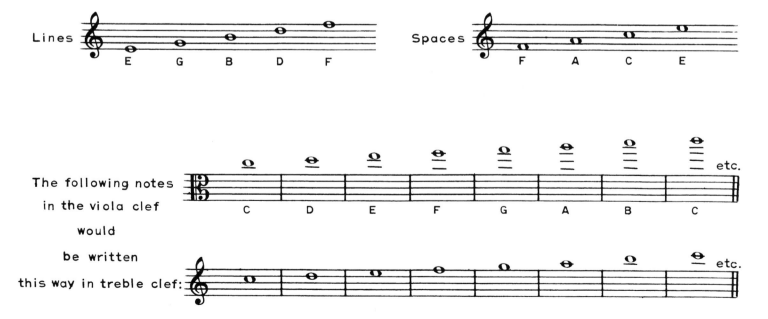

The two clefs alternate frequently in viola solos and orchestra music, therefore a number of exercises in this book will be devoted to the transfer of these clefs so that the student may become familiar with their usage.

Second Position
On the "A" String

Name all notes before playing.

Shift the whole hand from first position to second position. (Simply move up a whole step).

Note the key signature change.

Second Position on the D and A Strings

F Major Scale

Can you point out the half steps in this scale?

Practice different bowings.

Practice different bowings.

F Minor Scale

Point out the half steps.

Second Position on the G, D, and A Strings

B Major Scale

Waltz in B Major

Also practice playing this piece in the Key of Bb (2 flats).

B Minor Scale

Point out the half steps.

Bb Major Scale

Name the notes as you play.

Bb Minor Scale

Point out the half steps.

Second Position on the C String

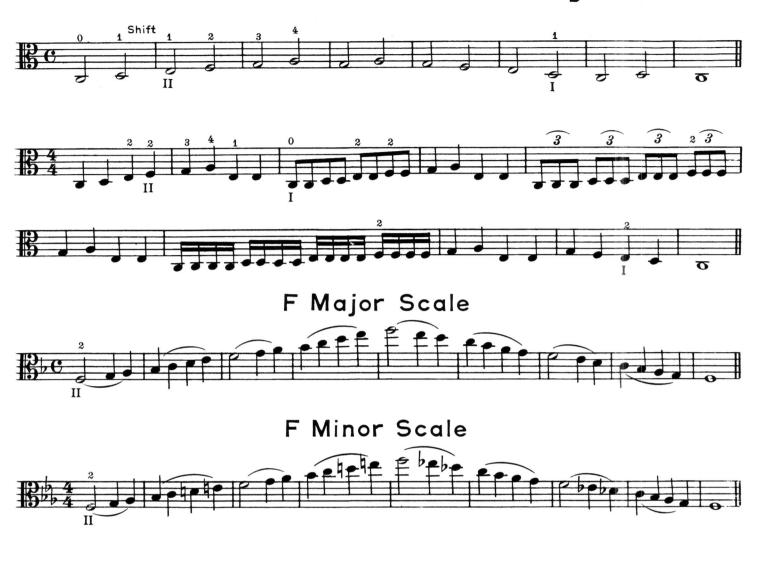

F Major Scale

F Minor Scale

Second Position Melody

Be sure to play your half steps and whole steps correctly.

Theme in F Major

Etude No. 8

poco ritard.

Third Position

Scales in Third Position

Be sure you know where the half steps are.

F Major

Gb Major

G Major

G Minor

F# Minor

Practice in Shifting

Keep the finger on the string as long as possible when shifting.

1st and 2nd finger shifts.

1st and 3rd finger shifts.

Shifting (Continued)

1st and 4th finger shifts.

Shifting from one string to another.

Ricochet Bowing

Etude No. 9

Ricochet or Thrown Staccato applies to two or more staccato notes connected in one bow. The upper part of the bow is used. The bow is raised and thrown on the string so that it is allowed to rebound the exact number of notes needed.

Practice the exercise in different ways, as follows:

28

Merry Dance

Etude No.10

Con spirito

Near the frog

Middle of bow

scherzando

Repeat previous
measure

III

Lento *pesante*

accel.

a tempo

Lento *pesante*

accel.

a tempo

829-47

The Harmonic

The Harmonic is a flute-like tone which is obtained by stopping the string lighty with the fingers. Natural Harmonics appear in various places in the string. The most commonly used is the octave harmonic which divides the string exactly in half from nut to bridge. This is usually played with the 4th finger by stretching up one whole-step from third position. The Harmonic is indicated by a cipher along with the finger to be used ($\frac{4}{0}$).

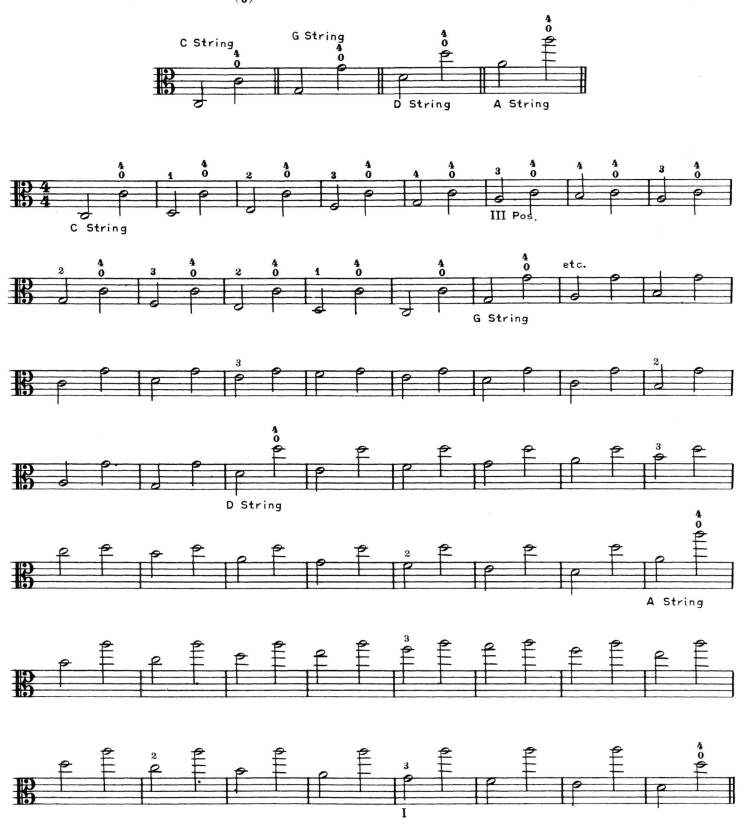

Playful Harmonics

Etude No. 11

Empire Builder

Etude No.12

In Olden Times

Etude No. 13

Slowly, in Minuet style

Triplets Play a Tune

Etude No. 14

Arpeggi
(Broken Chords)

Etude No. 15

Practice:
Separate bowing.
Two in a bow.
Three in a bow.
Six in a bow.

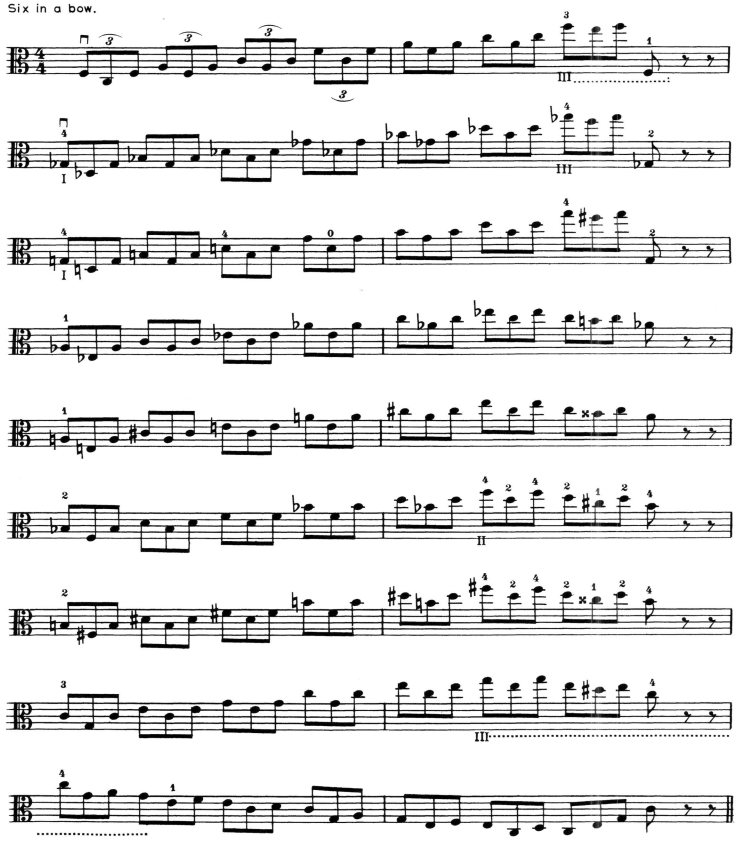

Breakwater

Etude No. 16

Freely

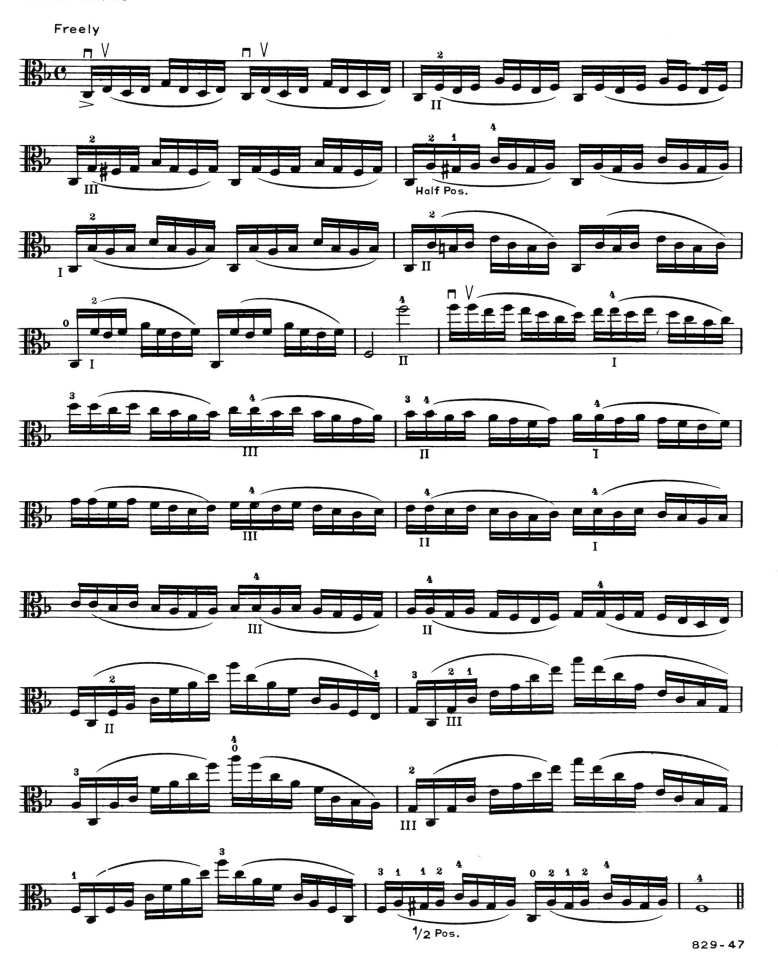

Concert Waltz

* Pizzicato. Sweep the strings with the forefinger of the right hand without changing the position of
the bow.

The Auto Race

Etude No. 17

Play slowly at first.

Introducing the Treble Clef (𝄞)

Review page 17

The Treble clef is confined mostly to the A string and should present no special difficulty if the notes are carefully learned. The treble clef is no more necessary in viola music than an extra clef would be in violin music (except for the slight advantage of avoiding leger lines on high notes) but must be learned in order to read foreign editions which use the clef frequently.

These notes in Viola clef,

are written here in Treble clef.

By examining the two lines above, you will notice that the treble clef brings the notes down into the staff, thus eliminating the leger lines. Study the notes and fingering carefully so you will be able to recognize them, and be able to play them when you see the change of clef in studies and solos.

Here is a 2-octave scale showing how the treble clef connects with the viola clef.

You start in viola clef then change to treble and keep on ascending on the A string.

Now come down the scale — It works the same way.

Watch this one. You change to treble clef before you reach the A string.

Three Familiar Melodies

Name the notes before playing.

G Major Scale. (Point out half steps)

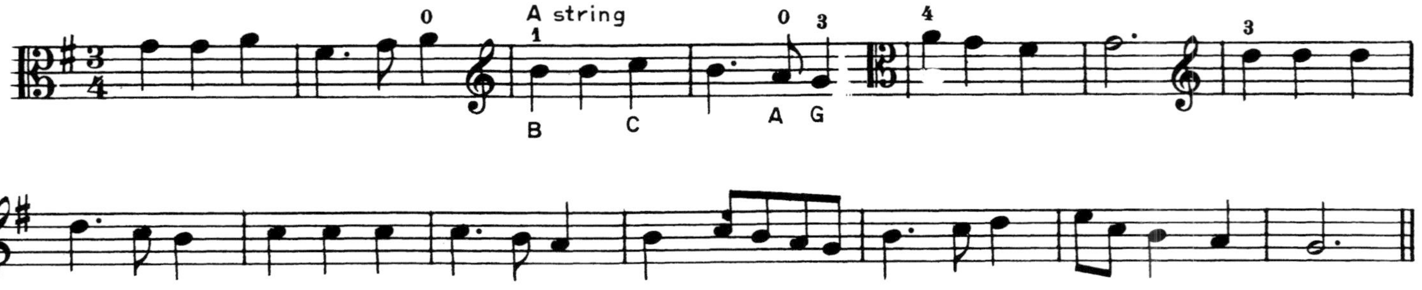

Fine (End)

D.S. al Fine

(Go back to % and
end at "Fine")
829-47

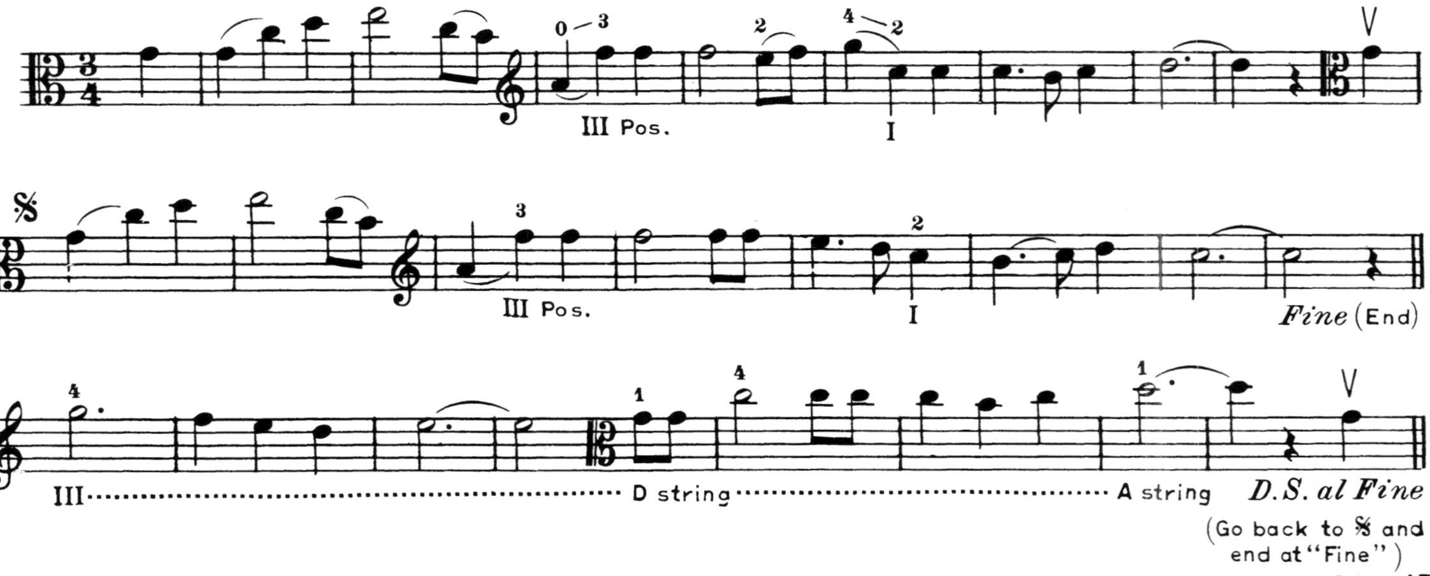

Professor Alto, Meet Doctor Treble!

Etude No. 18

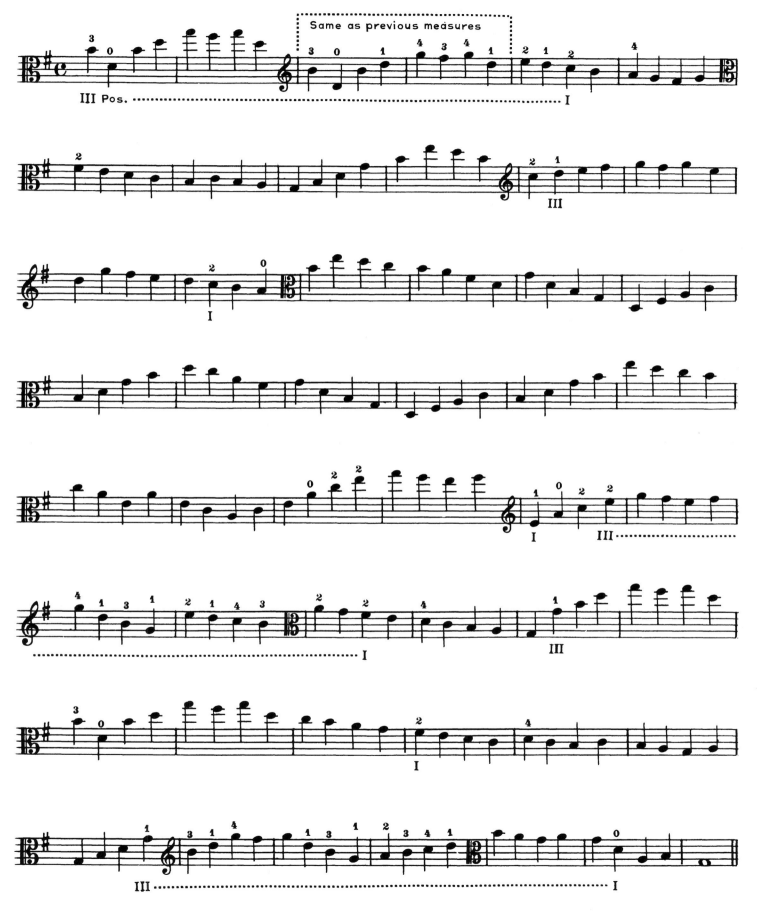

D Major Scale

Remember Playing This Before?

Etude No. 19

Name the notes before playing.

Syncopating Novelty

Etude No. 20

Intermezzo
Duet for Two Violas

Viola I

S.D.W.

Intermezzo

Duet for Two Violas

Viola II

S.D.W.

Rondo

Duet for Two Violas

Viola I

PLEYEL

Rondo

Duet for Two Violas

Viola II

Allegretto

PLEYEL

VOCABULARY OF TERMS AND EXPRESSIONS

Accelerando (Accel.) — Gradually faster.

Adagio — Slow.

Ad libitum (ad lib.) — At will.

Agitato — With agitation.

Alla breve — A change of 4/4 to 2/2 (cut time — 2 beats to a measure).

Alla marcia — In march style.

Allegretto — Light and cheerful.

Allegro — Fast.

Allegro con brio — Quick and brilliant.

Allegro con fuoco — Quick, with fire.

Allegro ma non troppo — Lively, but not too fast.

Allegro moderato — Moderately quick.

Allegro molto — Very quick.

Allegro vivace — Fast and lively

Al segno — To the sign, 𝄋

Andante — Slowly, but do not drag.

Andante cantabile — Slowly, in a singing style.

Andantino — Somewhat quicker than Andante.

Animato — With animation.

Appassionato — With intense expression.

Arco — With the bow.

Arpeggio — Playing chord tones in harp style.

Assai — Very.

A tempo — In time.

Calando — Gradually softer and slower.

Calmato — With a calm, tranquil expression.

Cantabile — In a singing style.

Coda — A passage or section which forms the close of a part or movement.

Colla parte — Following the principal part.

Colophone — Rosin.

Comodo — Easy, without haste.

Con brio — With spirit and vigor.

Con molto — Faster.

Crescendo (cresc.) — Gradually louder.

Da capo — Repeat from the beginning.

Da capo al fine — Repeat from the beginning to the sign "Fine."

Da capo al segno — Repeat from the sign, 𝄋

Decrescendo — Decrease in loudness.

Deciso — With decision.

Diminuendo (dim.) — Gradually softer.

Dolce — Softly, sweetly.

Doloroso — With sadness.

Espressivo — With expression.

Fermata (⌢), or Hold — A pause.

Finale — The last movement of a sonata or symphony.

Fine — The end.

Frosch — The nut of the bow.

Furioso — With fury.

Grandioso — With grandeur.

Grave — Slow and solemn.

Grazioso — With grace and elegance.

Lamentando — Mournfully.

Langsam — Slowly.

Larghetto — Slow, but not as slow as Largo.

Largo — Very slow and broad.

Legato — Smoothly, connected.

Leggiero — Light, easy.

Lento — Slow.

Maestoso — With majesty, dignity.

Maggiore — The major key.

Marcato — Marked.

Martelé — Hammered bow stroke.

Meno — Less.

Mineur — The minor key.

Moderato — In moderate time.

Molto — Much, very.

Morendo — Dying away.

Perdendosi — Decreasing in power and time.

Pesante — Heavily.

Piu mosso — Faster.

Pizzicato — Plucked string.

Poco — A little.

Poco a poco — Little by little.

Ponticello — To be bowed near the bridge.

Poussé — Up bow.

Prestissimo — Very fast.

Presto — Fast.

Prima vista — At first sight.

Rallentando (rall.) — Gradually slower.

Rapidamente — With rapidity.

Religioso — In a religious manner.

Ripieno — An added part in the orchestra to give more force in a Tutti.

Risoluto — With resolution.

Ritardando (rit.) — Gradually slower.

Ritenuto — Hold back.

Sautillé — Springing bow.

Scherzando / Scherzo — In a playful manner.

Segue — Follows; comes after.

Semplice — Simple, unaffected.

Sempre — Always.

Senza — Without.

Simile — In the same manner.

Smorzando — Dying away.

Sonore — Sonorous, with a full, rich tone.

Sordini, con — With mutes.

Sostenuto — Sustained.

Staccato — Detached; cut off; separated.

Stringendo — Suddenly faster.

Sul A — On the A string; **Sul D** — On the D string; etc.

Tacet — Silence.

Tenuto (ten.) — Sustain the note.

Tiré — Down bow.

Tranquillo — Calmly.

Tremolo — A note bowed with great rapidity so as to produce a quivering effect.

Tutta forza, con — With the greatest force.

Tutti — All; everybody.

Una corda — On one string.

Variazioni — Variations.

Vigoroso — Vigorously, boldly.

Vivace — Lively, quickly.

Vivo — Quick, brisk.

Volti subito (V.S.) — Turn quickly.